Playing with Worlds
an anthology of non-dual poems

by *Peter Baker*

These variations on a singular theme are
dedicated to the unnameable reader
– you know who you are

Other books by Peter Baker (available from Amazon):

Non-dual insights, enquiries and playthings.

*Tricks of the light – non-dual essayettes
        on thought, science, emptiness and subjectivity.*

Non-dual soundbites – postcards from no-mind's-land.

The author can be contacted at: *pbworlds167@gmail.com*

First published 2020
Copyright © 2020 Peter Baker

ISBN: 9798698287506
Independently published

"Finite players play *within* boundaries;
infinite players play *with* boundaries"
– James P Carse

Contents

The gift

There is a gift which can never be given.
I could give you a dried flower to keep forever
in your scrapbook of ideas,
or I could take you to a field
where one fleetingly dances with the wind
but can never be yours to own or hold.

Truth always dies before it can be spoken,
rather than become a withered but enduring lie.
This moment is the field in which it plays
in ever-changing forms,
alive, uncatchable and wild.

You are this wind, this field,
this flower and this truth, this gift.
A given - yet ungiveable,
unownable, unholdable,
untold.

This infinite moment

The fear of death is the
fear of this moment ending.
In the grip of fear we attempt
to capture this moment as it flows.
We call this the 'past'.
We attempt to capture this moment
before it arrives.
We call this the 'future'.
Dwelling in these captured times
this moment may seem lost.
Looking back and looking forward
this moment is overlooked.
Yet this moment doesn't really have
any time for reflection or projection.
This moment is not small but infinite,
it can't be found or lost.
This moment is alive and spacious.
Imagined 'death' can never touch it
but only remind us of its preciousness.

The undead

This silent space was haunted
by a million spectral selves
but there is no one who
believes in them anymore.
A peaceful presence has loved them all away.
They were nothing more than reflections
of imagined absence
and in the light of this moment
I have given up the ghosts.

Reflections

When you look back on your life you may
reflect on the choices that you made
and the choices that made you.
You may talk of the reasons why things
happened as they did and of what they
did when they happened.
But now, in this looking,
where have those choices gone?
What has happened to 'what happened'?
Except within the stories we tell
has anything really changed?

No path brought you here.
The trail you see is only a reflection
in this still and silent lake of looking.
Empty of reason, empty of choice,
empty even of the one who looks,
yet full of love,
reflected as all of this.

Unplaceable

I've realised that not only am I
not the man I used to be
but that I never was.

The person I thought I used to be
and the one I thought I may become
are simply appearing as this presence
only here
and just for now
in this land that can't quite be placed
at this moment that can't quite be measured
as this form that can't quite be defined
in these words that can't quite be spoken
to the you who can't quite be reached
as this no-thing and this no one
that can't quite be found
and never needs to be
anything but what
it is.

There's this

There's this
and there's pictures of this
and the pictures of this
are painted *by* this
and they're painted *with* this
they're the *image* of this
they're not other than this
but they're not quite the same
as this.

The time being

You appear to be an object
amongst many divided in time,
but you are really the infinite being
in which time is conceived.

When you appear to exist in time you suffer
the apparent separation of a 'time being'
of a being existing in time.
But this is only temporary,
it's only for the time being,
because beyond this appearance of division
there is always only you being whole.

At the 'end of the day'
when you know yourself as the beingness of time
you are no longer subject to it
nor an object in it.
You are only a 'time being' for the time being
but are always and timelessly being.

The empty mask

I wear a mask to disguise the fact
that I have no face.
It's not that I'm trying to hide my appearance
it's just that I don't have one.
When I wear it people seldom see the real me
but if I took it off they wouldn't even
know that I was there.
Who I really am beneath the skin will not be
revealed until you realise that this mask I wear
does not belong to me at all
- but to you.

Treading water

Adrift in this uncertain sea
through thoughts we swim
in desperate search
of shores which never show.
Thrashing around until
exhausted, we flail and fail
in forced surrender
only to find
that no one drowned
because no one swam.
Unthinkable
unsinkable
I am.

Getting there

We live with the dream of 'not yet'
but with the feeling we are 'getting there',
without realising that the one
who lives this dream
can never be anywhere else but here.
We try to sort all this out
before death sorts us out
without realising that there is nothing to sort.

This is the immaculate misconception
which is a forgetting and a remembrance.
And when it's remembered
then it's remembered right now
and it's remembered that
the forgetting doesn't matter
because forgetting is as harmless as
the mere idea of brokenness in wholeness.

We are like children that cry
at imagined monsters
whilst being in our mother's arms
and then awaken to the
peace of her embrace.

A goner

I disappeared for a moment
and in that moment there was no other moment.
Everything I thought I was or had fell away,
including the one who appeared to think it.
Standing in the place where I once stood
stood nothing
appearing to be everything.

I lost myself for a moment,
a moment not unlike this one,
and then it all came back to me,
or perhaps it was I that came back to it.
Whichever way it was
it was for no other reason
than the love of it.

And now I don't feel the same anymore.
I'm not the one I seemed to be.
So whilst apparently still being here
in this infinite moment
I'll always be
a goner.

Goldilocks

I'm liking the way things are appearing right now.
They are neither so heavy that they can't be
picked up and played with
nor so light that they float away.
They're like dream tigers
but they still need feeding.
I like it when things have just
the right amount of bite to them.

I'm liking the way people are appearing right now.
They are neither so different that I can't
have fun with them
nor so the same that they don't show up.
They're like friendly ghosts
but they can't walk through walls.
I like it when people have just
the right amount of person in them.

I'm even liking the way
my porridge is this morning.
It's not too lumpy and not too runny
It could be different - but it's not
And I wouldn't want it any other way.

Space-time tales

When and where can I find this 'I'
that I think myself to be?
Only in the storyline of my memory
and the imagination of my future.
In time gone by and yet to be.
Only in contrast to all of the places and
things that appear to be outside myself,
in spaces where I am not.
Only in thoughts of thoughts of time and
space apart from here and now.

What thoughts are *of* are never-present things.
What thoughts are *of* are simply thoughts,
no-where, no-when, no-things,
but what thought itself *is,*
is an ever-presence...
unthinkable, unfindable,
unhidden, and unmissable.

All of this

If there is a desire for awakening to take you
away from all of *this*
then get ready for a disillusionment.
In awakening what is taken away is not all of *this*
but all of *that* -
the idea that there could ever be or ever was
another way to be,
the idea that there could ever be or ever was
a start or an end to being,
the idea that there could ever be or ever was
someone who was asleep,
the idea that anything could ever be
added or taken away from *this*.
And when all of *that* goes,
then with it goes the desire
for anything other than all of *this*.

The secret

The mind always wants to know
and then wants to know a little bit more.
That's the mind's problem,
it never really knows what it wants.
It is only the heart that really knows,
and what it really knows
is that that the mind will never know
and never know the end of wanting,
and that's the heart's little secret -
that no one really knows
and no one really wants for anything.

Once upon a time

The problem is not that we make
stories out of things
but that we make things out of stories -
that our stories make assumptions about things
which don't exist outside of the stories.

Life leads us down the garden path
but there are no fairies at the bottom of
imaginary gardens.

No garden – no fairies.
No story – no things.
No self – no problems.

Unapparent

I am
not the thing that I appear to be
nor am I something else.
Some call me nothing.
Some say I'm everything.
But beyond the notion of anything
I am.

Reading between the lines

My heart writes
about something and nothing.
And as this keyboard is touched
and this love letter appears
and your heart reads
and your heart responds
then for a moment
this writer and this reader forget
who is writing and who is reading.
And in between these lines a light shines,
and dazzled, word-blind
in this infinite moment
what we thought defined us as others
simply melts.

Lost for words

When every possible combination of words
has eventually been written
in an attempt to explain what it's all about
and still failed,
will someone write a book containing
nothing but blank pages?
Or will they just invent more words to in order to
avoid the ineffable void
that threatens to engulf the
irrepressible wordsmith?

Elusive

I could tell you my name
but what would that really tell you
except what I call this idea of a self?

I could paint you a picture
of some flowers waving in the breeze
but what I really want to paint
is the breeze in which the flowers wave
but this always escapes my hand.

The word for the wordless is the one
I'd like to tell you.

Forgiven

There was a sense that all of the
ideas about my life
were mistakes.
A body had been born,
a self had been conceived
and everything else appeared to
support this assumption.
My mistake was in taking the world
to be other than the taker
and in taking this view to belong to me,
but this supposed self was never mine to take
and the mistake was never mine to make.
There was nothing about the named
that could separate it from the nameless.
The mistake was to think
I was a *taken*
not the *given*.
It was simply an innocent illusion
appearing to be guilty of something
that is now forsaken and forgiven,
now unbelieved
and overlooked by love.

The nothing that is

All there ever is, is this silent presence,
and presence can never be thinged or thought of.
The only things that can be thought of
are appearances
- thoughts of the presence of things
and thoughts of the absence of things.

All that is ever seen are sights.
All that is ever felt are feelings.
All that is ever spoken are words.
All that is ever experienced are experiences
and all these things come to nothing now.

All appearances are the
appearances of presence
yet presence cannot be known
by any particular appearance.
Presence will never come to you
but you will eventually come to presence.

Nothing is ever transmitted from silence
things simply fall into it.
Things dissolving into the
endless presence
of the nothing that *is*.

Seeming

At first the world and I were one.
The world was both the seen and the seer.
Then they told me that the
world wasn't really like that,
that it wasn't what I saw,
that it was being coloured by the way I looked.
That there was the world 'as it is'
and the world 'as I saw it'.
Two worlds then?
They were right in a way
because the world is not what it seems,
but they were wrong in a way
because it is nothing else
but the seeming.

The plaything of love

What would I be if I could act without purpose
live without meaning
dream without hoping
die without caring
and love without needing?

Where would I go if I could travel
without being driven?
If the meaningful and meaningless
became meaning-free?
If hopefulness and hopelessness
were free of hope?
If carefulness and carelessness
became carefree?

What would I be if there was
nothing left for me to do
and no need for the 'me' who
pretends to need or be anything?
Then the love for my self would be
unveiled as love in itself
and 'I' would be nothing but
the plaything of love.

And where could this be but here
and when could this be but now?
This infinite moment
this infinite love.

Wavicles

Sometimes I seem to be a particle.
Sometimes more like a wave.
It depends on whether I am splashing
and spluttering for dear life and trying
to keep the idea of my head above water,
or if there is nothing in particular appearing
and I am simply drifting around
and only waving – not drowning.

Give us this day

Every day
we know only wholeness
but think only separation,
until we come to see the trick of thought.
Then the presence of wholeness
embraces the appearance of separation
and loves it away.
And so this goes on
for no reason
but for love.

When all is said and apparently done,
we come to realise that
this love never was an option
that could be absent or refused
but is either thought of and concealed
or known of and revealed.
And this is the story of our lives,
over and over,
but never over.

Ripples

'I've heard ripples'
said one wave to another
'that this water is disturbed by
our incessant breaking
and longs for calm'.
'Don't get in a froth about it'
came the reply,
'this ocean's full of notions
but you'd never catch
the water saying that,
and though we may
fall and break ourselves
this never bothers the water'.
Upon hearing this
the wave was pacified
and the water was,
as ever,
silent.

As if a wave could talk!
Of course this is nothing
but a story of which
I've heard ripples.

The imaginary penny

Once upon a time
I thought I had a real self.
But then I found it was only an illusion
so I was left with an illusory self.
Then I lost the one that I
thought had had the thought
and the illusion too was gone.
Now all that's left is the knowing of this.

So the penny's finally dropped
and the penny that's dropped
is that there never was
a penny to drop.

Being the world

The world only has colour
because we have eyes.
It only has sounds
because we have ears.
It can only be touched
because we have feeling.
It only has smells
because we have noses.
It can only be tasted
because we have tongues.
And all of these things have their being
only in our awareness.
Where else could they possibly exist?
We do not sense the world
– we *are* the world.

Virtuality

A dream is the appearance of a virtual reality.
Reality is a dream that is not yet
recognised as such.
Waking up is not about seeing things
as they really are
but about seeing that things
really aren't.

It is not good news for the dreamer
who wants to become a waker
to find that all reality is virtual.

Things are not to be trusted.
They are devious little liars.
Not only are they never what they seem to be
but they're not anything else either.
And just like them I am neither
one thing nor another.

Playing around

Though I simply play a part in this
I sometimes play it so well
that I get lost in it
and forget that I am only playing
and begin to think that I really am a part.
But then I remember that there is nothing
apart from the whole
that sometimes appears
as this part
when it's playing around.

Deeper

It is quite usual to feel stillness when all is still
but more precious to find it in activity.

The peace of peacetime is a blessed relief
but as nothing to the peace which witnesses war.

The knowing of knowledge is useful to have
but the knowing of unknowing is far deeper.

The silence which softens noise is restful
but the silence that lives within it is purer.

It is a gift to be in love with your beloved
but the love that knows no other is sublime.

Beyond the light that lights the darkness
is the light that lights itself.

This Knowing

There may be the appearance of someone here
who is on a mission to discover their true nature,
the appearance of one who has forgotten
but who may someday remember.
There may also be the appearance of a world
of other somebodies like this one
and of ones who claim
to have already remembered.
There may also be the appearance of paths
which may eventually lead to this remembrance.

Meanwhile,
beyond all such appearances,
I merely *am*
but without the mereness
and with nothing to remember.
No mission,
no direction or reason
and no lack of them.

Nothing is necessary in order to *be*,
but neither my seeming body
nor the other somebodies who may appear
can ever know this
because appearances
cannot know anything.

The known can never know
but this Knowing always is.
And whatever may appear
all this Knowing ever knows is
This.

The appearance of knowing this may fade
but the Knowing as which it appears remains,
not throughout all time
but beyond it.

By whatever name it is called
and as whatever form it takes,
this Knowing can never really be remembered
because it has never really been forgotten.

The so-called 'duck'

There is something in the canal.
It looks like what they call a duck.
It swims like what they call a duck,
and it quacks like what they call a duck.
But what is it?
It's probably what they call a duck.
But what is that?
And who are they?
And what am I?
Duck knows – I don't!

Carrying on

Everyone carries a banner.
Some use it to proclaim their own particular truth
and to bash others around the head with.
Some people wave banners saying
'This is not a banner'
but you'd still better watch your head
as they walk by.
Some people have banners saying
'This is only a banner'
and they use them to bash *themselves*
around the head with
just in case they forget they are carrying one.
Yes life can be painful at times
but everyone secretly loves it.
My banner just says 'Ouch!'
but I wouldn't want things differently.
Some people say I'm a sucker for punishment
but everyone carries something,
and my banner is made of light.

Untold

When I look within I seem to glimpse
a half-formed thing
composed of looking,
that apparently walks a half-formed path
composed of walking,
but on refection there is
nothing to be found but reflections.

And when I tire of wandering around in thought
both the looking and appearing fade away
and what remains cannot be named,
and nor can I.
For I am that which is
(just like a story prior to the telling)
untold.

Travelling light

Do not run from the heartbreak
nor be shy of the ecstasy.
Do not dwell in the darkness
nor cling to the light.
But live as the play
between falling and flight.

The teaser

What better disguise could I take
than to appear as every single thing
and as all of the spaces in between
overlooked due to my obviousness?

As both the silence and the noise.
As both the darkness and the light.
As the particle, the wave and the observer.
The parting, the waving and the seeing.
The unmissable appearing as the unfindable.
As all of these things yet not as any one of them.

'But why go under cover?' you may ask.
'Why play so hard to get?'

Well how else would you expect me to appear?
What could appearance be except a show
- the façade of Being?
It's funny how what something looks like
gets taken for what it is,
either that or for being something else.

When the chase is over you will see
that I was hidden only when
you searched for me,
or rather that it wasn't I that hid but you
by assuming the mask of a seeker.

But who are you to ask anyway?
And who am I to answer?
We are not two.
I am not one.
I am.

Unquestioning

She asked if he had loved her at first sight.
'Oh no' he said, 'I didn't start to love you then'.

She asked if he had loved her when he first
heard her speak.
'No' he said, 'I didn't begin to love you then
either'.

She asked if he had loved her when he found out
what she was really like.
'No' he said, I can't say that I did, because when I
first saw you I couldn't believe my eyes, and on
hearing you speak I couldn't believe my ears, and
I am yet to discover if I can really trust your
likeness'.

She asked if this meant that he had never loved
her at all.
'Oh no' he said, 'it means my love for you knows
no beginning and will know no end. When my first
breath was taken it was in the midst of your love
and my body will die in it too.
But of course, being the one behind my
breathing, I know your questions can only be in
play because you already know the answers. It is
I that sometimes needs reminding.

They say some things

They say that Eskimos have over
50 words for snow.
That's nothing, I have
10 thousand words for the unnameable!

They say it's a fine life
so long as you don't weaken
but I've found it's even finer if you do.

They say that we're a long time dead
but I don't even remember being born.

They say things aren't the way they seem
but I've found that they're nothing but that.

They say some things don't they!
but I'm not too sure about
the tales that people tell
and I'm not even sure of my own.

So here I am – all dressed up
but with nowhere to go
and with so many words
and yet nothing to say.

'Is that a thing?'

Things appear distinctly only
when viewed from a certain distance.
Move closer and they become fuzzier.
Touch them and they begin to melt.
Love them and they disappear.
But their disappearance is no real loss.
For what disappears as a thing
remains as the Self.
There's no need to shed a tear
when an illusion dies.

Undivided

My thinking mind says:
'First there was the world.
Then I was born into it
and someday I will die in it.
During my time here my awareness
comes and goes.
It is punctuated by gaps
called deep sleep.'
On the other hand
direct experience just says:
'I am, I am, I am.'
only without the commas
and without the repetition
and without the full stop
and even without the saying.
Unpunctuated
unrepeatable
unspeakable
undying
unborn
I am

Unidentified

It seems that there is no true identity to be found
just the melting away of false ones
which arise only to fall
in this.
And that melting is what we know as the love
which dissolves the lines we draw -
'loves them away' like your mother's kiss did
to your imagined pains
which arose purely so as to invite her lips.
Imagined so as to be forgotten
so as to be remembered,
yet ever present, never lost.
How could we ever want this to end?
How could we ever ask for more than this?

Dissolving

When you think of me
you hold me in your thoughts
when you look at me
you hold me in your sight
when you question me
you hold me in your doubt
when you speak to me
you hold me in your words
but when you love me
you release me from your hold
and we melt
as one
in love.

Faking it

If there were no real world
I would make one out of thought,
and take it with a pinch of salt,
just for the taste of it,
just for the love of it.

And so, it would appear in thought -
a world not in any way unlike this one.

And then, so that it seemed to matter more
(whilst knowing that it couldn't matter less)
I'd lose myself in the drama of this world
and let myself be carried away by metaphors,
a self-shaped ship adrift in a sea of others.

And if someone asked me
how everything came to be the way it seemed
I could easily deny all knowledge.
And if (in so-called time)
the questions got too much
I'd say
'Just who do you think you're talking to?'
and they'd say
'I've really no idea, that's why I ask'
and I'd say
'Hmmm... so let me look'
and then I'd wonder
'Who am I?'

Then after a bit more 'time'
in a moment not in any way unlike this one,
when the appearance was wearing thin,
being world-weary and exhausted
by the iffyness of dreams,
I'd remember
and awaken.

Yes, that's what I'd do
if there were no real world.

Listening

Objects are the notes in the music of awareness.
But if you listen closely enough to these notes
you may no longer hear them
as both they and you melt into the music.
Were they ever really there?
Were you ever really not?
And such, they say, is the sound
of one hand clapping.

A tissue of lies

She said 'The Universe is made of stories,
not of atoms.'
And these stories are made of words
which are made of letters,
signifying signs.
Painting pictures,
making music
dancing dancers,
running rings,
telling tales,
thinking thoughts
living lives
and dying deaths.
A tissue-ing
atishoo-ing
they all fall down.

Unbrokenness

I hear the wind is blowing in the trees,
yet it looks like the trees are blowing in the wind.
Being infinite I appear to be finite,
being nothing I appear to be something,
being alive I worry about dying.
But brokenness is just the way
unbrokenness appears to be
when looked at from a distance,
when you're six feet tall
and you have two eyes
and a head.

Nothing to speak of

There's nothing which sees or is seen
just seeing.
There's nothing which thinks or is thought
just thinking.
There's nothing which is or is not
just appearing.
There's nothing which you are or are not
just being.
There's nothing which is aware or to be aware of
just awaring.
And while speaking of nothing,
there's nothing to speak of
just saying.

Unborn

There can be the knowing or
the not knowing of things
and of the self which appears
to know or not know things
but there is no alternative
to the knowing of Knowing itself.

There is always and only this Knowing
whether or not this is known.
The self that you think you are is not immortal
but it is the knowing of that self which is the
true eternal one.
Selves come and go just like all thoughts do
as the appearances of the knowing
that you always are.
All beings will eventually cease to exist
but the beingness you are can never die
as it was never born.

Discoveries

I've found out that when I loosen
my grip on things
they also loosen their hold on me.
When I stop taking the world so literally
it also stops taking me so seriously
and when I wink at it – it winks back
just like that self I see in the mirror does.

And something thing else I've discovered
is that this breath that breathes me…
it's so much more
than molecules.

The story of this and that

There's a this that depends on that.
And this this comes and goes
and when this comes so does that
and when this goes so does that
and when this comes back it thinks
it is the same this that went away
because it seems to have brought back
all of the same thats with it.
But this this can never be
the same as that this
because that this is just an
appearance in this this
and when this this goes
all that remains is nothing
and this nothing is everything
and the only thing that comes back
is the story of this and that
appearing in the This that never leaves.

Enough

I am not that which changes
nor that which remains the same.
I was not here in the past
nor will I be here in the future.
I am not found during sleep
nor do I arise in wakefulness.
Difference and sameness,
past and future,
sleeping and waking,
these all reside in me.
I am neither temporary
nor permanent.
I have nothing
so lack nothing
and that
is enough.

Coming to rest

My life used to swing
from the sublime to the ridiculous.
Now it's just ridiculously sublime.

It was simply deceptive.
Now it's deceptively simple.

I used to be aware of nothing.
Now Nothing's aware of me.

No other

There being no other times,
there is no time.
There being no other places,
there is no place.
There being no other selves,
there is no self.
There being no other things,
there are no things.
yet there being no other being
there is only being.

Story of my life

Once upon a time I was born,
or so I've been told.
They dressed me and named me
and taught me how to behave
like everybody else.

Soon I was the new boy in school
and the teacher told me to sit at the
spare desk for the present.
So I sat at that desk for ages
but she never gave me a present.

Soon I went to work where the grown up people
do important things to make their living
and the manager told me to sit in an
office for the time being.
So I sat in that office, a being in time,
until they said it was my time to leave.

Soon I'll be the old boy in a care home
and the nurse will tell me to sit in a chair
and wait there to die or for supper,
whichever comes first.
So I'll sit in that chair until
they say my time is up.
They'll say I've had a good innings
and now face my final outing.
It's time for the happy ending
or so they'll tell me.

Well that's the story
- but I don't believe a word of it.
All I've ever heard is hearsay.
Something never comes from nothing
and something never goes to nothing
except in fairy tales,
for things have always been nothing at heart
and I have never known any coming or going
no matter what they say.

You may think I am the teller of this story
but that would be telling
and I am not a teller of tales.

Unlonging

The changing longs for constancy.
The constant longs for change.
But awareness is neither changing nor constant
since it is free of duration.
In movement it appears as stillness.
In stillness it appears to move.
But it is neither moving nor still
since it is free of form.
Wanting for nothing
this is unlonging.

Love never minds

'Never mind' my mother used to say
when I fell and hurt myself,
'let me love it better'.
But I always minded too much,
so she couldn't make it better.

She's gone now,
her mind left first
and then her body died.
But 'never mind'
I hear her say,
'my love for you remains
and it's never too late for love
to make things better'.

Minding dies but love goes on
and never minds.

Something and nothing

There are many ways of talking
about this infinite and silent presence.
There are many ways of taking this
but all of them mis-takes.
There are many shallows here
which when stacked up
give an appearance of depth.
But remove the bottom card
from a house of concepts
and they all come tumbling down.
It's all done with
smoke and mirrors
by a mind that is itself
no more than
something and nothing.

Having words with the Goddess

'I know you created all this and you love it'
he said, 'but everything has to end sometime'.

'No I didn't' she said, 'so no, it doesn't'.

'But nothing lasts forever' he said.

'Yes it does' she said,
'it's the only thing that does'.

'You're thinking of the nothing that isn't' she said,
'I'm talking about the nothing that is'.

'Now you're just playing with words' he said.

'No, you take them too seriously' she said,
'I'm playing with worlds'.

'I was just saying' he said.

'I know' she said, 'and I'm just playing.
You think of this world as a real thing' she said,
'I think of it as a play and the play's the thing.'

'If you say so' he said.

So she let him have the final word but
the play went on …as it does.

Huang Po said

'If you conceive of a Buddha,
You will be obstructed by that Buddha!'

He could just as well have said this...

If you conceive of a Christ,
You will be obstructed by that Christ image!

If you conceive of an Allah,
You will be obstructed by that idea of Allah!

If you conceive of a God,
You will be obstructed by that God image!

If you conceive of Awareness,
You will be obstructed by that Awareness!

If you conceive of Enlightenment,
You will be obstructed by that Enlightenment!

Conceptions veil the inconceivable.

We are often too busy looking at the trees
to see the forest.

Beyond all ways

There are many ways of being
Like being a prince or being a frog
Being a body or being a mind
Being awake or being asleep
Being alive or being dead
Being here or being there
Being this or being that.
Being everything or being nothing.
So what do they all have in common?
You already know the answer -
they're all ways of being.
But being itself is beyond all ways.
It simply is.

There are many ways of being
and no way of not being.
You are all-ways being
and beyond all ways
you simply are.

The mistaken thought

A thought assumed I was a 'thing'
a thing that had a thought
a body that was labelled 'me'
a 'thing' that thinks!
how could that be?

Losing face

I finally decided to face my fate,
there being nothing else for me to face.
Then with nowhere else for it to fall,
everything that fell, fell into place.
And in a moment infinite and sweet,
My self dissolved in a loving space.

Unsensible

Who am I?
In looking with my eyes
I see only what is visible.
In listening with my ears
I hear only what is audible.
In thinking with my mind
I conceive of only thoughts.

How could who I am ever be
found by the senses?

I am the source of seeing
but I am invisible.
I am the source of hearing
but I am inaudible.
I am the source of concepts
but I am inconceivable.
I am the source of the finite
but I am infinite.
I am the source of all things
but I am not a thing.
I am what remains
when the questioner leaves.

Self-sufficiency

Enough water in my bucket.
Wanting no more
I am rich.

The look of love

Whenever there is seeing I become visible.
Whatever is seen at this moment
this is what I look like.
Whenever there is hearing I become audible.
Whatever is heard at this moment
this is what I sound like.
If I were never visible
then there would be no sight.
If I were never audible
then there would be no sound.
Whenever appearances arise
then whatever form they take
this is how I appear.
These sights, sounds and appearances
are only misleading if they
are thought to exist apart from me.
My being is infinite
my appearance finite.
It would be a mistake to judge me
by the way that I appear
and yet another one to deny that I do so.
If I were not,
then there would be no appearances.
But sometimes there are
and always
I am.

Don't even go there

The place where thought can never go
is the place it can never leave.
So don't be surprised if you can't place it.
It's somewhere that can't be placed
because there's nowhere else.

You can't find it
it's unlocatable.
You can't miss it
it's unavoidable.
It's neither here nor there.
You *are* it - it's *you*.
You're home.

Revelation

This reveals that,
that reveals this.
Nothing reveals everything,
everything reveals nothing.
Background reveals foreground
foreground reveals background.
The play's the thing
the thing's the play.
I am not a thing
but I am revealed by things.
I am not the way I seem to be
but I am revealed by this seeming.
In appearing, things are.
In being, things appear.
Appearances are revealed by being.
Being is revealed by appearing.
Things, in seeming, are being.
Being, in seeming, is things.
The parts reveal the whole.
The whole reveals the parts.
Being is given, appearance is taken.
The given is taken, the taken is given.
However I appear,
I am being.
What a revelation!

Mirror image

I looked into the mirror.
Who can that person be?
I remember - it's a mirror
There is no one there but me.
It's not one I really am
but just the one I see.

Musing

If I had my whole body replaced bit by bit
at what point would I cease to be me?
And when that happened would it be a surprise?
Maybe it's already happened?
Maybe it never stops happening?
Maybe I'll never end?
Maybe I never began?
Maybe I'm irreplaceable
and irreducible?

Madland

There is a fictional land
where many mortal beings live.
They spend their lives
trying to achieve immortality.
They live like frightened guests
at their own parties,
always afraid that the host is
going to throw them out.
Little do they know that there is
nowhere to be thrown.
You don't have to be mad to live there but
(as you've no doubt heard so many times)
it helps.

Ping-pong

The ever-changing appearance
and the never-changing presence
are the 'what it looks like' and the 'how it feels'.
Neither dependent nor independent,
they are not two.
When this is - that is.
When that is - this is.
The appearance of presence
is the presence of appearance.

It takes two to tango
but there's only one dance.
It's a game of two halves
but there's only one game.
So you can serve and I'll return.
Ping-pong!

Like nothing else

Sounds like
a bird is singing
looks like
a song is birding
seems like
a world is selfing
feels like
a self is worlding
but *being* is like
no such happening
and is like neither one thing
nor another.

Dry up

How better could I describe that which
is not two and is not one?
A knowing-being?
A thought-thing?
A will-o'-the-wisp of this love-hate relationship
that I have with this ironic world of words
in which 'hyphenated' has no hyphen
and yet 'non-hyphenated' does?
Maybe it's best not to say anything
but I think that it's too late for that
so I'll just keep going
until the words
dry up.

Seeing through seeing

To see things as they really are
is to see that there are no real things.
To see the essential self
is to see that there are no essential selves.
To see who you truly are
is to see that truly you are not.
To see yourself as a complete non-entity
is to see yourself as everything.
And when this is seen
then there is nothing more to see
but the seeing goes on.

The imaginary forest

I asked her if a tree were to fall in a forest
and there was no one there to hear it whether
it would still make a sound.
She said that first she would need to make
sure there was a tree and a forest.
She's practical like that.
I said it was a thought experiment
so she'd just have to imagine them.
'So let me get this straight', she said,
'you want to know if an imaginary tree
in an imaginary forest would make
a sound if it fell?'
She thought for a bit and then said,
'I imagine it would but if I were you
I wouldn't take the word of a character in
a poem who only seems to be aware.
You're gullible like that – you make your world
and then you tell lies in it.'
'Now here's a question for you' she said,
'If the universe ends in a poem and there's
no one there to read it, would it go out
with a bang or with a whimper?'
Before I could answer she was gone
and all that remained
was a deafening silence.

Ding-dong

What I am I do not know
But *that* I am I know is so
What I am I cannot say
But *that* I am is clear as day
What I am I is hard to tell
But *that* I am rings like a bell.

Complicating simplicity

How to complicate this simplicity:
Call yourself a Buddhist when
even the Buddha wasn't one of those.
Use an exotic word when
a plain one would be just as good.
Dress in special clothes though they're
all made of the same thread.
Make a big thing out of this when
it's not even a little one.
Fly a flag to display your colours though
the wind itself is colourless.
Write a book about how this
can never be put into words.
Disagree with how others express this
though there are no others.
Think about this instead
of simply being it.
Pretend that this simplicity could
ever become complicated.
Even say any of this when you could
simply share a smile.

Rampant imagination

Wholeness imagined separation in order
to appreciate its own existence,
but unfortunately for Wholeness it was
separation that stood out the most.
Is-ness imagined isn't-ness in order
to celebrate its own presence,
but unfortunately for Is-ness it was
isn't-ness that got all of the attention.
No-thingness imagined things in order
to express its own creativity,
but unfortunately for no-thingness it was
things that really caught the eye.
Presence imagined absence in order
to recognise its own being,
but unfortunately for Presence it was
absence that made all the headlines.
That's what happens when you let your
imagination run away with you.

Freedom

A wave is not free in the ocean until
it sees itself as the ocean,
A flame is not free in the fire until
it sees itself as the fire,
A breeze is not free in the wind until
it sees itself as the wind,
You are not free in this until
you see yourself as this.

Pointless

Here I am,
attempting to point at what is pointing,
by looking at what is looking,
and then talking about what is talking.
How can I possibly point to where I am
unless I'm somewhere else?
And when I'm already in the only place there is
surely all signposts are equally misleading.
So what's the point of pointers?
You can't get to here from here.
You have to go somewhere else first,
and then find your way back again.
You'll just have to pretend to travel though,
because there's nowhere else to go.

Beyond

Appearances are often called the unreal.
Awareness is often called the real.
But the unreal is the appearance of the real
and the real appears as the unreal.
Where are such distinctions to be found
except in thought?
Beyond both somethingness and nothingness
what conclusions can be reached?

Spaciousness

This spaciousness can be neither
grasped nor contained.
Even fear cannot restrict this presence
which embraces all contraction.
This spaciousness, being ever present,
can never be re-presented.
And it can never be remembered,
because it has never been forgotten.
This spaciousness, being everything,
is seen by nothing,
known by nothing
and *is* no 'thing'.
You are this presence that knows
no self or other.
You are this moment that has
no beginning or end.
You are this aliveness that breathes life
into every appearance.
You are this spaciousness that
can never be found
because it has never been lost.

Comforter

My 94 year old mother
was crying out this afternoon.
She kept asking me where her father was.
She sobbed and pleaded with me to find him.
Her mind can no longer explain away her pain.
My mind though, with its reasoning,
still comforts me.
Is that what minds are for,
to placate imaginary selves
and pretend they are still there?

Trickster

Never trust those who say they tell the truth
for the truth cannot be told.
Believe me on this
for I would never lie to you.
The next sentence is true.
The previous sentence is false.
So don't believe a word I say.
Trust me, you cannot trust me.

Teacherless

My teacher died
but I'm a student still.
Of whom I do not know.
Of what I cannot tell.

The only lover

This moment is the only lover
that will never leave you.
Even though denied and scorned,
it still embraces you.
This is all you'll ever long for,
and all you'll ever have.
No matter what it looks like,
you are already absorbed by
this presence
in which every fear dissolves.

Turtality

Your turtle 'self' is perched unaware
on the backs of stacks of turtle 'others'
all with remembered turtle 'pasts' behind
and imagined turtle 'futures' ahead.
All turtles think they swim alone,
not knowing that they carry an
infinity of turtles on their shells
and ride infinite turtles beneath.
Moving as one through nothingness
turtles squashed between turtles
all thinking they are turtle kings.
Because of their restricted view,
their crusty shells,
no turtle ever realises that it's
turtles all the way up
and turtles all the way down.
There's nothing but turtles
yet not a 'single' turtle to be found
only the Turtality.

Intimacy

It's too close to see
but it looks like it's seeing.
It's too close to touch
but it feels like it's feeling.
It's too close to hear
but it sounds like it's singing,
It's too close to tell
but it breathes like it's breathing.
It seems like it's 'you-ing',
and then like it's 'me-ing'.
It's both and it's neither,
It's life simply be-ing!

Awareness

Awareness is everything you think Awareness is not.

Awareness is everything you think Awareness is.

Awareness is everything you think.

Awareness is everything.

Awareness is.

Awareness.

Unthinking

Think of a self.
Now add the idea of seven billion others.
Think about their seven billion secrets
their seven billion worlds.
Now take away the one you first thought of
How many are left?
Not two, not even one.
Do the math
then undo it.

Picture this

You wonder what this is.
This is completely obvious
and totally unavoidable.
Whatever you are seeing through your eyes,
that is what this looks like.
Whatever you can hear right now,
that is what this sounds like.
The gentle breeze on your face,
that is what this feels like.
The aroma of coffee waiting to be sipped,
that is the scent of this.
The sharp, sweet orange on your tongue,
that is the taste of this.

This is appearing as everything,
so all descriptions are descriptions of this
and all experiences are experiences of this.
So immediate, so clear, is the picture of this.
You know exactly what this is like.
You know all there is to know of this,
and everything about it.
Yet often overlooked is what this *is,*
that which is described
that which is experienced,
no amount of of-ness or aboutness
comes close to this.

Lovelight

The one you think you are dies
in the space between each thought.
Appearing only as long as the
cartoon frames flicker.
Animated only by the illusion
of reflection and projection
like the remembrance of an absence,
like a trick of the light.
A film featuring ten thousand images
dancing without motion,
whilst through their static forms
the presence of infinity shines,
breathing life into the story
and love between the lines of self
which flutters like a moth defying death,
then flying into the fiery flames
which first denies then
simply dies for love.

Unbelievable

Only by lying,
can I avoid contradiction.
To tell you the truth,
I must constantly change my story.
Only lies can be believed in,
the truth goes by too quickly.
Lies need thinking about
but the truth can't wait that long.
You can die in eternal lies
or live in the transient truth.
All be-lie-fs have a lie in their heart.
So don't be-lie-ve a word,
they're re-lie-ably
lie-able
to lie.

The veils of love

Love loves cloudiness just as much
as it loves sunniness.
Resist the clouds and they
appear to be opaque.
Love them and they
become transparent
Because even the clouds
are made from love.
And everything is as it is meant to be
although without the 'meant'.
And everything is as it should be
although without the 'should'.
And even the veils of love
are made from love.

Heart breaking open

If you worry about life being lost
remember that all that can ever be lost
is the illusion of loss
and the one who apparently worries.

When the world breaks your heart open
only then will it be realised that there is
no one left to suffer
and nothing is ever broken.

Life births you and breathes you
then breaks you and takes you
back to where you never left.

Already

Already eternal,
not pretending to be something that isn't
but simply being the nothing that is.
Not anything
but everything
intertwingled,
luminous,
complete.

Paradoxica
(some bite-sized, relentless reprisals)

I used to think I was seeing *things*
but then I realised I was only *seeing* things.

If it's a thing it's not real
if it's real it's not a thing.

I may *think* that I know things
but I only *know* that I think things.

Things are not the way they appear to be
they are the appearance of the way.

There is no seeing things as they really are
as in themselves, there are no such things.

Everything matters
but nothing *really* matters.

It doesn't *have* to be like this
it's just that there's no alternative.

There are no sentient beings
only the being of sentience.

That you are is a given
what you are is a taken.

There's no getting around this
because *this* is always around you.

I found that somethingness was really nothing
but that nothingness was really something.

There is no time without presence
but there may be presence without time.

After all is said and done
you will still be untold and undone.

The bottom line is that there is no bottom line.

No regrets

There may come a time when you regret
not having done more.
Then later there may come a time when you
regret wasting even that time on regrets.
Then there may be a moment when there will
no longer be any time for regrets
and there will be nothing to regret.

This moment that I speak of is not the one
in which your death arrives but a moment,
just like this one,
in which time dies,
the idea of death dissolves
and in which life has always flowed.

Not over yet

This isn't the end.
How could the eternal
come to an end?

So don't hold your breath,
it will never be over
until 'over' is over
and the infinite lady sings.

Printed in Poland
by Amazon Fulfillment
Poland Sp. z o.o., Wrocław